Brothers at War: A History of the India-Pakistan Conflict

Copyright Page

TITLE: Brothers at War: A History of the India-Pakistan Conflict

1ST Edition

Copyright @ 2023

ISBN: 9798223682240

Table of Contents

Brothers at War: A History of the India-Pakistan Conflict

By Roberto Miguel Rodriguez

Chapter 1: Fighting Brothers; The History of the Enmity Between India and Pakistan

Historical context of the India-Pakistan conflict

The India-Pakistan conflict is a deeply rooted and complex issue that has its origins in a long and tumultuous history. Understanding the historical context is crucial for diplomats, mediators, and religious leaders seeking to address this protracted conflict.

The enmity between India and Pakistan can be traced back to their shared history as part of the British Raj. In 1947, when India gained independence from British colonial rule, the subcontinent was divided into two separate nations: India, with a Hindu majority, and Pakistan, with a Muslim majority. The partition of the subcontinent resulted in widespread violence, displacement, and communal tensions, laying the foundation for the ongoing conflict.

Border disputes and territorial conflicts have been a significant source of tension between India and Pakistan. The dispute over Kashmir, a region with a majority Muslim population but under Indian control, has been a central point of contention. Both countries have fought several wars and engaged in military confrontations over Kashmir, leading to a cycle of violence and animosity.

Cultural and religious differences have also fueled the enmity between India and Pakistan. India is predominantly Hindu, while Pakistan is an Islamic republic. These differences, coupled with a history of communal violence, have deepened the divide between the two nations and hindered efforts towards reconciliation.

The role of British colonialism in shaping India-Pakistan relations cannot be understated. The British policy of divide and rule sowed the seeds of religious and communal tensions, making it easier to maintain control. The legacy of this strategy continues to impact India-Pakistan relations, with both countries blaming each other for the communal violence that occurred during the partition.

Economic rivalry and competition have further exacerbated the conflict. India and Pakistan have often engaged in trade disputes and economic competition, with each country striving to gain a competitive edge. This economic rivalry has added another layer of complexity to the already strained relationship.

The nuclear arms race between India and Pakistan has also intensified the conflict. Both countries possess nuclear weapons, raising concerns about the potential for a catastrophic escalation. The presence of nuclear weapons adds an element of urgency to resolving the conflict and highlights the need for international interventions and mediation.

The international community has played a significant role in attempting to mediate the India-Pakistan conflict. Numerous peace initiatives and mediation efforts have been made, but a lasting resolution has remained elusive. The complexity and deeply ingrained nature of the conflict make it challenging to find a mutually acceptable solution.

The impact of the India-Pakistan conflict on the Kashmir region cannot be ignored. Kashmir has been the epicenter of violence and suffering, with its residents caught in the crossfire between India and Pakistan. The conflict has led to a loss of lives, displacement, and human rights abuses, exacerbating the already fragile situation in the region.

Efforts towards peace and reconciliation between India and Pakistan have been made over the years. Diplomatic negotiations, confidence-building measures, and peace talks have been undertaken, but progress has been slow and often marred by setbacks. However, it is vital to recognize and support these initiatives as they offer hope for a peaceful resolution to the conflict.

In conclusion, the historical context of the India-Pakistan conflict is crucial to understanding the roots of this ongoing enmity. Border disputes, cultural and religious differences, the role of British colonialism, economic rivalry, nuclear arms race, international interventions, and the impact on the Kashmir region are all key factors that shape this complex conflict. By delving into this historical context, diplomats, mediators, and religious leaders can gain deeper insights and work towards a lasting peace and reconciliation between the two nations.

Border disputes and territorial conflicts between India and Pakistan

Border disputes and territorial conflicts between India and Pakistan have been a central issue in the long-standing enmity between these two nations. The history of these conflicts is intricate and layered, with roots that extend far back into the colonial era and the partition of British India.

The border disputes between India and Pakistan primarily revolve around the regions of Jammu and Kashmir, which have been fiercely contested by both sides. These conflicts have resulted in several wars, including the Indo-Pakistani War of 1947-1948, the Indo-Pakistani War of 1965, and the Kargil War of 1999. These military confrontations have not only claimed thousands of lives but have also left lasting scars on the Kashmir region.

The cultural and religious differences between India and Pakistan have played a significant role in fueling the enmity between the two nations. India, with its Hindu majority, and Pakistan, with its Muslim majority, have had contrasting approaches to governance and societal structures. These differences have often been weaponized by political leaders to rally support and justify their territorial claims.

The role of British colonialism cannot be understated in shaping India-Pakistan relations. The arbitrary drawing of border lines during the partition of British India in 1947 created a legacy of territorial disputes that continue to this day. The hasty division of the region and the subsequent mass migration led to immense violence and displacement, leaving wounds that have yet to heal.

Economic rivalry and competition have also been significant factors in the India-Pakistan conflict. Both nations have sought to outdo each other in various sectors, including agriculture, industry, and technology. This economic competition has further fueled the animosity between India and Pakistan, as each side perceives the other as a threat to its progress and development.

The nuclear arms race between India and Pakistan has added a dangerous dimension to the conflict. Both nations possess nuclear weapons, raising concerns about the potential for a catastrophic escalation. The international community has been actively involved in urging restraint and promoting nuclear non-proliferation in the region.

Efforts towards peace and reconciliation between India and Pakistan have been ongoing, with various international interventions and mediation attempts. Diplomats and mediators have played a crucial role in facilitating dialogue and negotiations between the two nations. However, achieving lasting peace remains a formidable challenge due to deep-rooted historical grievances and unresolved territorial disputes.

The India-Pakistan conflict has had a profound impact on the Kashmir region, which has become a symbol of the larger dispute. Kashmir has been marred by violence, insurgency, and political instability for decades, with the local population caught in the crossfire. The conflict has severely affected the socio-economic development of the region and has led to widespread human rights abuses.

In conclusion, the border disputes and territorial conflicts between India and Pakistan have been a complex and multifaceted issue. Understanding the historical context, cultural and religious differences, and the role of external factors such as colonialism and international interventions is crucial for diplomats, mediators, and religious leaders seeking to contribute to peace and reconciliation between these two nations. Efforts towards peace must address not only the territorial disputes but also the underlying grievances and aspirations of the people involved. Only through sustained dialogue and genuine efforts at understanding can a lasting resolution be achieved.

Cultural and religious differences fueling the enmity between India and Pakistan

Cultural and religious differences have played a significant role in fueling the enmity between India and Pakistan. These differences have deep historical roots and have been exacerbated by various factors over time. Understanding the cultural and religious dynamics is crucial for diplomats, mediators, and religious leaders seeking to address the India-Pakistan conflict.

India and Pakistan, despite being neighboring countries, have starkly different cultural and religious identities. India, with its diverse religious landscape, is predominantly Hindu, while Pakistan was founded as a homeland for Muslims. This religious divide has led to a sense of mistrust and competition between the two nations, as each seeks to protect and advance the interests of their respective religious communities.

Historically, the partition of India in 1947 further deepened the cultural and religious differences between the two countries. The violent and traumatic events surrounding the partition, including widespread riots and mass migrations, left lasting scars on both nations. This traumatic experience created a sense of animosity and distrust that continues to shape the India-Pakistan conflict today.

Border disputes and territorial conflicts have also been fueled by cultural and religious differences. The disputed region of Kashmir, for example, is a predominantly Muslim area that has been a major point of contention between India and Pakistan. Both countries claim the region as their own, leading to multiple wars and ongoing tensions.

The role of British colonialism cannot be overlooked when examining the cultural and religious differences between India and Pakistan. The British Empire's policy of divide and rule exacerbated existing tensions and fostered a sense of separateness between Hindus and Muslims. This colonial legacy has had lasting effects on the India-Pakistan relationship.

Additionally, economic rivalry and competition have further aggravated the cultural and religious differences between the two nations. Both India and Pakistan strive for economic development and regional influence, often viewing each other as obstacles to their goals. This economic rivalry has fueled hostility and contributed to the ongoing conflict.

Religious leaders, diplomats, and mediators must recognize and address these cultural and religious differences to effectively navigate the India-Pakistan conflict. By acknowledging and respecting the diverse cultural and religious identities of both nations, and promoting dialogue and understanding, there is hope for peace and reconciliation between India and Pakistan. Efforts towards peace and reconciliation should aim to bridge the divide caused by cultural and religious differences, promoting tolerance and mutual respect. Only through a comprehensive understanding of these dynamics can a lasting resolution to the India-Pakistan conflict be achieved.

The role of British colonialism in shaping India-Pakistan relations

The deep-rooted enmity between India and Pakistan can be traced back to the colonial era when the British ruled over the Indian subcontinent for nearly two centuries. The legacy of British colonialism has had a profound impact on the relationship between these two nations, shaping their history, politics, and even their cultural and religious differences.

During the partition of India in 1947, the British hastily divided the country along religious lines, creating India as a predominantly Hindu nation and Pakistan as a Muslim-majority state. This hasty and poorly executed partition led to mass migrations, communal violence, and the displacement of millions of people. The scars of this traumatic event can still be felt today, as it set the stage for a long and bitter conflict between the two newly formed nations.

The British colonial rulers also played a significant role in exacerbating the territorial disputes between India and Pakistan.

They drew arbitrary borders, dividing regions and communities, without considering their historical, cultural, and ethnic ties. This led to the creation of several contentious border issues, most notably the dispute over the region of Kashmir. The British left the issue unresolved, and it has since become a major flashpoint between the two countries, resulting in several wars and ongoing tensions.

Furthermore, the British colonial administration favored certain religious and ethnic groups, creating a sense of discrimination and marginalization among others. This fostered a deep-seated mistrust and animosity between communities, which continues to fuel the enmity between India and Pakistan to this day.

Economically, British rule further accentuated the divide between India and Pakistan. The colonial administration prioritized certain regions, investing in infrastructure and industries that favored British interests. This created economic disparities between the two nations, leading to a sense of rivalry and competition that persists even after independence.

The nuclear arms race between India and Pakistan can also be attributed, at least in part, to British colonialism. The British conducted nuclear tests in the region during their rule, laying the groundwork for the development of nuclear capabilities by both India and Pakistan in later years.

In conclusion, the role of British colonialism in shaping India-Pakistan relations cannot be understated. From the hasty partition to the unresolved territorial disputes, the legacy of colonial rule continues to cast a long shadow over the relationship between these two nations. Understanding this historical context is crucial for diplomats, mediators, and religious leaders seeking to resolve the deep-rooted conflicts and build a lasting peace between India and Pakistan.

Chapter 2: Economic Rivalry and Competition between India and Pakistan

Economic disparities and their impact on India-Pakistan relations

The economic disparities between India and Pakistan have played a significant role in shaping their complex and often tumultuous relationship. This subchapter aims to shed light on the impact of these disparities and how they have influenced the India-Pakistan conflict. It is addressed to diplomats, mediators, and religious leaders who play a crucial role in fostering peace and reconciliation between the two nations.

The economic rivalry and competition between India and Pakistan have been fueled by their shared history and territorial conflicts. The partition of India in 1947 led to the division of resources, with Pakistan receiving a smaller share. This disparity in wealth and resources has created a sense of resentment and a desire for economic dominance between the two nations.

The role of British colonialism cannot be ignored when analyzing the economic disparities between India and Pakistan. The British Empire left a legacy of economic inequality, with India being the center of economic power and Pakistan struggling to catch up. This imbalance has had a lasting impact on their relations and has contributed to the ongoing conflicts.

Furthermore, the nuclear arms race between India and Pakistan has had a profound impact on their economic development. Both nations have spent significant resources on their military capabilities, diverting funds away from social and economic development. This arms race has not only heightened tensions between the two countries but has also impeded their ability to address pressing economic issues.

The impact of the India-Pakistan conflict on the Kashmir region cannot be overstated. The disputed region has suffered from economic stagnation and underdevelopment due to the ongoing conflict. The constant military confrontations and wars between India and Pakistan have resulted in a lack of investment and economic opportunities for the people of Kashmir.

Efforts towards peace and reconciliation between India and Pakistan have been hampered by these economic disparities. It is imperative for diplomats, mediators, and religious leaders to address these economic grievances and work towards creating a more equitable economic relationship between the two nations. Only by addressing these disparities can we hope to pave the way for lasting peace and stability in the region.

In conclusion, the economic disparities between India and Pakistan have had a profound impact on their relations. The history of enmity, border disputes, and cultural differences have all been exacerbated by economic rivalry and competition. It is crucial for diplomats, mediators, and religious leaders to recognize the role of economic disparities and work towards creating a more balanced and equitable relationship between the two nations. Only through addressing these economic grievances can we hope to achieve lasting peace and reconciliation in the India-Pakistan conflict.

Trade disputes and competition for resources between India and Pakistan

Trade disputes and competition for resources between India and Pakistan have long been significant factors in the ongoing conflict between the two nations. This subchapter explores the economic rivalry and its implications, providing historical context and highlighting the impact on various aspects of the India-Pakistan conflict.

Throughout history, economic competition has played a critical role in exacerbating tensions between India and Pakistan. Both countries vie for control over resources, including water, minerals, and agricultural land. The scarcity of these resources, combined with the population growth in both nations, intensifies the competition and heightens the potential for conflict.

One of the key catalysts for trade disputes between India and Pakistan is the issue of water resources. Several major rivers flow through both countries, including the Indus and the Ganges. The sharing of these rivers has been a subject of contention, with each side accusing the other of unfair water usage. These disputes not only impact the agricultural sector but also have significant implications for the livelihoods of millions of people.

Trade barriers and tariffs have further fueled the economic rivalry between India and Pakistan. Both countries have implemented protectionist policies, hindering free trade and impeding economic growth. These barriers create a hostile environment for trade and investment, exacerbating the already strained relations between the two nations.

Moreover, competition for resources extends beyond water and trade. The nuclear arms race between India and Pakistan has also been influenced by economic considerations. Both countries have invested heavily in their respective nuclear programs, diverting significant resources that could have been utilized for socio-economic development. This arms race has exacerbated tensions and increased the risk of a catastrophic conflict.

International interventions and mediation have been crucial in addressing these trade disputes and economic rivalries. Diplomats and mediators have played a pivotal role in facilitating dialogue between India and Pakistan, advocating for peaceful resolutions and promoting economic cooperation. Religious leaders have also been instrumental in fostering understanding and reconciliation between the two nations.

Efforts towards peace and reconciliation have included initiatives to enhance economic cooperation, such as the establishment of free trade zones and the promotion of cross-border investments. These endeavors aim to create mutually beneficial relationships and alleviate economic grievances that contribute to the conflict.

In conclusion, trade disputes and competition for resources have been significant factors in the India-Pakistan conflict. This subchapter provides insights into the economic rivalries between the two nations, highlighting the impact on various aspects of the conflict. It emphasizes the need for international interventions, mediation, and efforts towards peace and reconciliation to address these issues and promote a more stable and prosperous region.

Attempts at economic cooperation and integration

In the tumultuous history of the India-Pakistan conflict, there have been several noteworthy attempts at economic cooperation and integration between the two nations. These efforts, although often overshadowed by the deep-seated enmity and political disputes, have demonstrated the potential for shared prosperity and peaceful coexistence.

One of the earliest attempts at economic cooperation occurred shortly after the partition in 1947. Recognizing the interdependence of their economies, India and Pakistan signed the Bilateral Trade Agreement in 1948. This agreement aimed to facilitate the exchange of goods and services between the two countries, despite the ongoing border disputes and territorial conflicts. However, the agreement faced numerous challenges due to the fragile political climate and was eventually suspended.

Throughout the years, there have been sporadic attempts to revive economic cooperation. In the 1960s, the two nations signed the Indo-Pakistani Protocol on Trade, which aimed to liberalize bilateral trade and reduce tariff barriers. However, this initiative was short-lived as tensions escalated, leading to the Indo-Pakistani War of 1965.

In the late 1980s, both India and Pakistan underwent significant economic reforms, opening up their markets to foreign investment and trade. This period witnessed a renewed interest in economic cooperation, with the establishment of the Indo-Pakistan Joint Business Council. The council aimed to promote trade and investment between the two nations and explore opportunities for economic integration. However, progress was hindered by political instability and the subsequent Kargil conflict in 1999.

Despite these setbacks, there have been some notable achievements in recent years. In 2012, India and Pakistan took a significant step towards economic cooperation with the signing of the Pakistan-India Trade Normalization Agreement. This agreement aimed to normalize bilateral trade relations, streamline customs procedures, and expand the list of tradable items. Additionally, both countries have made efforts to improve transportation infrastructure and facilitate cross-border trade.

While these attempts at economic cooperation and integration have faced numerous challenges, they serve as a reminder of the potential for shared prosperity and peaceful coexistence between India and Pakistan. The diplomats, mediators, and religious leaders involved in the India-Pakistan conflict must recognize the importance of economic cooperation in fostering stability and reducing tensions. By promoting trade, investment, and economic integration, there is a possibility of building trust and paving the way for lasting peace and reconciliation in the region.

Chapter 3: Nuclear Arms Race between India and Pakistan

Origins of the nuclear arms race in the region

The nuclear arms race between India and Pakistan is a significant aspect of the broader India-Pakistan conflict, rooted in a complex web of historical, cultural, and geopolitical factors. Understanding the origins of this arms race is crucial for diplomats, mediators, and religious leaders seeking to resolve the conflict and promote peace in the region.

Historically, the enmity between India and Pakistan can be traced back to the partition of British India in 1947, which led to the creation of two separate nations along religious lines. The border disputes and territorial conflicts that followed further deepened the mistrust and animosity between the two countries. The unresolved issue of Kashmir, a region claimed by both India and Pakistan, has been a major flashpoint, fueling tensions and military confrontations.

Cultural and religious differences also play a significant role in perpetuating the India-Pakistan conflict. The predominantly Hindu India and Muslim Pakistan have often viewed each other through the lens of religious identity, leading to deep-seated biases and prejudices. These differences have been exploited by political leaders to rally support and maintain their grip on power.

British colonialism played a crucial role in shaping India-Pakistan relations. The British drew arbitrary borders and sowed the seeds of division, leaving behind a legacy of mistrust and unresolved territorial disputes. The economic rivalry and competition between the two countries, aggravated by the partition, further exacerbated the tensions.

The nuclear arms race between India and Pakistan emerged as a result of these complex factors. Both countries sought to assert their regional dominance and ensure their security in a volatile neighborhood. The acquisition of nuclear weapons became a matter of prestige and deterrence. India's first nuclear test in 1974 and subsequent tests by both countries in 1998 only intensified the arms race, raising concerns about the potential for a catastrophic nuclear conflict.

International interventions and mediation have played a crucial role in managing the India-Pakistan conflict. Various countries and international organizations have attempted to facilitate dialogue and find peaceful solutions. However, the deep-rooted mistrust and unresolved issues have often hindered progress towards lasting peace.

The impact of the India-Pakistan conflict on the Kashmir region has been profound. The disputed territory has witnessed decades of violence, human rights abuses, and a heavy military presence. The quest for self-determination by the Kashmiri people remains a central issue that needs to be addressed for a sustainable resolution.

Efforts towards peace and reconciliation between India and Pakistan continue despite the challenges. Track II diplomacy, cultural exchanges, and people-to-people initiatives have helped create spaces for dialogue and understanding. It is crucial for all stakeholders, including diplomats, mediators, and religious leaders, to support and encourage these efforts to promote lasting peace in the region.

Development of nuclear capabilities by India and Pakistan

The development of nuclear capabilities by India and Pakistan has been a significant factor in the India-Pakistan conflict. This subchapter explores the history, implications, and impact of the nuclear arms race between these two nations.

India's journey towards nuclear capability began in the 1950s, partly driven by its desire for self-reliance and concerns over security threats from its neighbors. It conducted its first nuclear test, codenamed "Smiling Buddha," in 1974. This development alarmed Pakistan, which felt the need to match India's nuclear capabilities to ensure its own security. Consequently, Pakistan embarked on its own nuclear program, leading to the successful detonation of its first nuclear device in 1998.

The acquisition of nuclear weapons by both India and Pakistan exacerbated the existing tensions between the two countries. The nuclear arms race added a dangerous dimension to the conflict, as it increased the potential for catastrophic consequences in the event of a military confrontation. It also raised concerns among the international community about nuclear proliferation and the potential for these weapons to fall into the hands of non-state actors.

International interventions and mediation have played a crucial role in managing the nuclear standoff between India and

Pakistan. Diplomats and mediators from various countries and international organizations have made efforts to promote dialogue, confidence-building measures, and non-proliferation agreements between the two nations. The aim has been to prevent a nuclear conflict and encourage nuclear disarmament.

The development of nuclear capabilities has had a profound impact on the Kashmir region, a major flashpoint in the India-Pakistan conflict. The presence of nuclear weapons has further complicated the already volatile situation in Kashmir, as it increases the risks associated with any military escalation or cross-border conflict.

Efforts towards peace and reconciliation between India and Pakistan have been hindered by the nuclear factor. The possession of nuclear weapons has instilled a sense of security and deterrence in both countries, making them less willing to engage in meaningful dialogue or compromise. However, it is essential for diplomats, mediators, and religious leaders to continue their efforts towards peace, as the consequences of a nuclear conflict would be devastating for both nations and the entire region.

In conclusion, the development of nuclear capabilities by India and Pakistan has deeply influenced the India-Pakistan conflict. It has added a dangerous dimension to the enmity between these two nations and further complicated efforts towards peace and reconciliation. The international community, including diplomats, mediators, and religious leaders, must continue to work towards promoting dialogue, confidence-building measures, and nuclear disarmament to ensure long-term peace and stability in the region.

Implications and risks of nuclear weapons in the India-Pakistan conflict

In the subchapter "Implications and risks of nuclear weapons in the India-Pakistan conflict" of the book "Brothers at War: A History of the India-Pakistan Conflict," it is crucial to address the implications and risks associated with the possession of nuclear weapons by both India and Pakistan. This chapter is specifically aimed at diplomats, mediators, and religious leaders who play a pivotal role in resolving conflicts and promoting peace in the region. It also caters to the interests of those interested in understanding the historical context, border disputes, cultural and religious differences, and economic competition that have fueled the enmity between the two nations.

The possession of nuclear weapons by India and Pakistan has had far-reaching implications, both regionally and globally. The threat of a nuclear exchange between these two countries poses a grave risk to the stability and security of South Asia. The potential use of nuclear weapons in the India-Pakistan conflict would result in catastrophic humanitarian consequences, causing widespread destruction, loss of life, and long-term environmental damage. It is vital for diplomats, mediators, and religious leaders to recognize the gravity of this risk and work towards preventing any escalation to nuclear warfare.

The role of international interventions and mediation in the India-Pakistan conflict is also a significant aspect to consider. The international community has a responsibility to promote peace and stability in the region by facilitating dialogue and negotiations between the two nations. Diplomats and mediators can play a crucial role in reducing tensions, building trust, and promoting confidence-building measures. It is essential for them to engage in sustained efforts towards de-escalation and disarmament, encouraging both India and Pakistan to adopt responsible nuclear policies and enhance non-proliferation measures.

Furthermore, the impact of the India-Pakistan conflict on the Kashmir region cannot be ignored. This long-standing dispute has led to human rights violations, militarization, and political instability in the region. Diplomats, mediators, and religious leaders must recognize the urgency of finding a peaceful resolution to the Kashmir issue, addressing the aspirations of the Kashmiri people, and ensuring their participation in any peace process.

Ultimately, the subchapter aims to emphasize the dire consequences of a potential nuclear conflict between India and Pakistan. It urges diplomats, mediators, and religious leaders to actively engage in efforts towards peace and reconciliation, encouraging dialogue, promoting confidence-building measures, and advocating for disarmament and non-proliferation. Only through sustained international cooperation and a genuine commitment to peace can the risks associated with nuclear weapons in the India-Pakistan conflict be mitigated, ensuring a secure and stable future for the region.

Chapter 4: Role of International Interventions and Mediation in the India-Pakistan Conflict

Early attempts at international mediation in the conflict

In the turbulent history of the India-Pakistan conflict, there have been numerous instances of international mediation aimed at resolving the deep-rooted enmity between these two nations. This subchapter delves into the early attempts made by various actors to mediate and find a peaceful solution to the long-standing dispute. It is particularly relevant for diplomats, mediators, and religious leaders who are invested in understanding the historical context and exploring potential avenues for reconciliation.

The India-Pakistan conflict dates back to the partition of British India in 1947, which led to the creation of India and Pakistan as separate nations. The immediate aftermath of partition was marred by communal violence, resulting in the displacement of millions and the loss of countless lives. Recognizing the need for intervention, the United Nations dispatched a mediator, Sir Owen Dixon, in 1950 to negotiate a solution to the Kashmir dispute, which had become a major flashpoint between India and Pakistan.

Sir Dixon's efforts, however, were met with limited success due to the deep-seated mistrust and conflicting claims of both nations. The subsequent years saw a series of military confrontations and wars between India and Pakistan, further exacerbating the enmity between them. Despite these challenges, international mediation continued, with countries like the United States, the United Kingdom, and the Soviet Union attempting to broker peace.

One significant milestone in this early mediation process was the Tashkent Declaration of 1966. After the Indo-Pakistani War of 1965, Soviet Premier Alexei Kosygin played a pivotal role in bringing Indian Prime Minister Lal Bahadur Shastri and Pakistani President Ayub Khan together in Tashkent, Uzbekistan. The declaration signed at Tashkent called for a ceasefire and the restoration of diplomatic relations between the two nations.

While the Tashkent Declaration provided a temporary respite, it did not address the underlying causes of the conflict. Subsequent attempts at mediation, such as the Simla Agreement of 1972 and the Lahore Declaration of 1999, also failed to achieve lasting peace. However, these early mediation efforts laid the groundwork for future initiatives, highlighting the importance of dialogue, negotiation, and compromise in resolving the India-Pakistan conflict.

It is crucial for diplomats, mediators, and religious leaders to study these early attempts at international mediation. By understanding the historical context and the challenges faced, they can gain insights into the complexities of the conflict. Armed with this knowledge, they can contribute to future peace-building efforts and work towards fostering understanding, dialogue, and reconciliation between India and Pakistan.

Role of the United Nations in resolving India-Pakistan disputes

The United Nations (UN) has played a crucial role in attempting to resolve the long-standing disputes between India and Pakistan. As diplomats, mediators, and religious leaders, it is important for you to understand the UN's involvement in this conflict, as it provides a valuable framework for peace and reconciliation.

The historical context of the India-Pakistan conflict is rooted in the partition of British India in 1947, which led to the creation of two separate nations – India and Pakistan. Since then, both countries have been engaged in border disputes and territorial conflicts, fueled by cultural and religious differences. This enmity has been further exacerbated by economic rivalry and the nuclear arms race between the two nations.

Recognizing the need for international intervention to prevent further escalation, the United Nations has actively mediated between India and Pakistan. The UN Security Council has passed multiple resolutions, urging both nations to resolve their disputes peacefully and encouraging them to engage in dialogue. The UN has also appointed special envoys and mediators, such as the United Nations Military Observer Group in India and Pakistan (UNMOGIP), to monitor ceasefires and facilitate negotiations.

One area where the India-Pakistan conflict has had a significant impact is the disputed region of Kashmir. The UN has been involved in the Kashmir issue since the 1950s, deploying peacekeeping forces and advocating for a plebiscite to determine the region's future. However, despite these efforts, a lasting resolution has remained elusive, and the conflict in Kashmir continues to be a source of tension between the two countries.

Throughout the years, there have been several military confrontations and wars between India and Pakistan. The UN has consistently called for an end to hostilities and has encouraged both nations to engage in diplomacy and peaceful negotiations. The UN's role in promoting peace and reconciliation cannot be overstated, as it provides a neutral platform for dialogue and fosters an environment conducive to resolving conflicts.

Efforts towards peace and reconciliation between India and Pakistan have been ongoing, and the United Nations continues to play a vital role in supporting these initiatives. It is through international interventions and mediation that progress can be made in resolving the disputes between these two nations.

In conclusion, the United Nations has been instrumental in attempting to resolve the India-Pakistan conflict. Its role as a mediator, facilitator, and advocate for peace has provided a framework for dialogue and reconciliation. As diplomats, mediators, and religious leaders, your involvement and support in these efforts can contribute to a peaceful resolution and a brighter future for both nations.

Efforts by regional and global powers to mediate the conflict

In the tumultuous history of the India-Pakistan conflict, regional and global powers have played a significant role in attempting to mediate the deep-rooted enmity between these two nations. Diplomats, mediators, and religious leaders have all made valiant efforts to bring about peace and reconciliation in this long-standing feud.

One of the earliest interventions came from the United Nations, which established the United Nations Commission for India and Pakistan (UNCIP) in 1948 to mediate the Kashmir dispute. The UNCIP proposed a plebiscite to determine the region's future, but the plan was never implemented due to the lack of consensus between India and Pakistan. Despite the failure of the UNCIP, their efforts laid the foundation for future mediation attempts.

Over the years, various regional powers have also stepped in to broker peace between India and Pakistan. One notable example is the Simla Agreement of 1972, facilitated by the Soviet Union, which aimed to resolve the issues arising from the 1971 Indo-Pakistani War and establish a lasting peace. The agreement led to the mutual recognition of the Line of Control in Kashmir and opened the path for future dialogue.

Global powers, such as the United States and China, have also exerted their influence to mediate the conflict. The U.S. has been actively involved in promoting peace talks between India and Pakistan, particularly during periods of heightened tensions. The Clinton administration's efforts in the late 1990s, known as the Lahore Declaration, aimed to deescalate the nuclear arms race between the two countries and foster greater cooperation.

Religious leaders have also played a crucial role in promoting dialogue and understanding between India and Pakistan.

Interfaith initiatives, such as the Aman ki Asha (Hope for Peace) campaign, have brought together religious leaders from both nations to promote peace, harmony, and mutual understanding.

Despite the numerous efforts, the India-Pakistan conflict persists, with sporadic military confrontations and territorial disputes. However, the consistent involvement of regional and global powers in mediating the conflict provides hope for a peaceful resolution in the future.

For diplomats, mediators, and religious leaders engaged in the pursuit of peace between India and Pakistan, it is essential to understand the historical context, cultural and religious differences, and economic rivalries that fuel the enmity between these two nations. By acknowledging these complexities, and building on past mediation efforts, there is a greater chance of finding common ground and fostering a lasting peace in the region.

Chapter 5: Impact of the India-Pakistan Conflict on the Kashmir Region

Historical background of the Kashmir dispute

The Kashmir dispute has been at the heart of the India-Pakistan conflict and has played a significant role in shaping the enmity between these two nations. To fully understand the complexities of this dispute, it is crucial to delve into its historical background.

The origins of the Kashmir dispute can be traced back to the partition of British India in 1947. At the time, the princely states were given the option to join either India or Pakistan, or remain independent. Kashmir, a predominantly Muslim state with a Hindu ruler, became a contentious issue. The ruler, Maharaja Hari Singh, initially chose to remain independent but soon faced internal unrest, prompting him to seek military assistance from India.

This move triggered Pakistan to intervene, as it had hoped to incorporate Kashmir due to its Muslim majority. The conflict escalated into the first Indo-Pakistani war, resulting in a divided Kashmir. The Line of Control (LoC) was established, dividing the region into Indian-administered Jammu and Kashmir and Pakistani-administered Azad Kashmir.

The religious and cultural differences between India and Pakistan have further fueled the enmity over Kashmir. India, with its predominantly Hindu population, has viewed Kashmir as an integral part of its secular identity. Pakistan, an Islamic state, sees itself as the natural guardian of Kashmiri Muslims and their right to self-determination.

The role of British colonialism in shaping India-Pakistan relations cannot be overlooked. The British Raj used a policy of divide and rule, sowing the seeds of communal tensions that persist to this day. The hastily drawn borders during the partition left many disputes unresolved, including that of Kashmir.

The economic rivalry and competition between India and Pakistan have also contributed to the conflict. Both nations have sought to outdo each other in various sectors, from agriculture to industry, resulting in a fierce competition for resources and influence.

The nuclear arms race between India and Pakistan has added a dangerous dimension to the conflict. Both nations possess nuclear weapons, creating a constant threat of escalation that could have catastrophic consequences for the entire region.

International interventions and mediation have played a crucial role in attempting to resolve the India-Pakistan conflict. Various diplomatic efforts, led by countries such as the United States, China, and the United Nations, have sought to find a peaceful solution and prevent further military confrontations.

The impact of the India-Pakistan conflict on the Kashmir region has been devastating. The ongoing violence, human rights abuses, and displacement of civilians have created a humanitarian crisis. The people of Kashmir have borne the brunt of this conflict, enduring decades of instability and uncertainty.

Despite the military confrontations and wars between India and Pakistan, there have been efforts towards peace and reconciliation. Numerous peace initiatives, such as the Lahore Declaration and the Shimla Agreement, have been signed in an attempt to find a lasting solution to the Kashmir dispute. However, these efforts have often been marred by mistrust and a lack of political will.

In conclusion, the historical background of the Kashmir dispute is a complex web of factors including border disputes, cultural and religious differences, colonial legacies, economic competition, and nuclear weapons. Understanding this background is crucial for diplomats, mediators, and religious leaders seeking to resolve the India-Pakistan conflict and bring peace to the region. Only through a comprehensive understanding of the historical context can meaningful progress towards peace and reconciliation be achieved.

Human rights violations and the Kashmiri struggle for self-determination

In the ongoing India-Pakistan conflict, one of the key issues that has plagued the region is the human rights violations and the Kashmiri struggle for self-determination. This subchapter aims to shed light on the atrocities committed in the Kashmir region and the urgent need for a resolution that respects the rights of the Kashmiri people.

The disputed region of Kashmir has been a focal point of tension between India and Pakistan since their independence from British colonial rule in 1947. The majority-Muslim region is divided between the two countries, with both claiming it as their own. In the process, the Kashmiri people have suffered immensely, with their basic human rights being violated on a regular basis.

Human rights violations in Kashmir have included extrajudicial killings, enforced disappearances, torture, sexual violence, and arbitrary detentions. These violations have been carried out by both state and non-state actors, with impunity and little regard for international norms and laws. The Indian security forces have been accused of using excessive force against protesters, leading to civilian casualties and further exacerbating the conflict.

The Kashmiri people have long expressed their desire for self-determination and the right to choose their own political destiny. However, their voices have often been silenced or suppressed through violence and intimidation. The struggle for self-determination has been met with a heavy military presence, curfews, and internet shutdowns, creating an environment of fear and oppression.

It is crucial for diplomats, mediators, and religious leaders to recognize the significance of addressing these human rights violations and the aspirations of the Kashmiri people. By understanding the historical context and the cultural and religious differences between India and Pakistan, they can play a pivotal role in facilitating dialogue and finding a peaceful resolution to the conflict.

International interventions and mediation efforts have had some success in de-escalating tensions between the two countries in the past. However, a comprehensive and lasting solution will only be achieved by addressing the human rights concerns and ensuring the right to self-determination for the people of Kashmir.

In conclusion, the human rights violations in the Kashmir region and the struggle for self-determination are critical aspects of the India-Pakistan conflict. Diplomats, mediators, and religious leaders should prioritize these issues in their efforts towards peace and reconciliation between the two nations. By acknowledging and addressing the grievances of the Kashmiri people, a path towards a just and lasting resolution can be forged, bringing much-needed stability and peace to the region.

External involvement in the Kashmir conflict

The Kashmir conflict, a long-standing territorial dispute between India and Pakistan, has attracted significant external involvement throughout its history. This subchapter explores the role of international interventions and mediation in the India-Pakistan conflict, providing insight for diplomats, mediators, and religious leaders.

The Kashmir conflict dates back to the partition of British India in 1947, when the princely state of Jammu and Kashmir was given the choice to join either India or Pakistan. The decision of the Hindu ruler to accede to India led to a military intervention by Pakistan, triggering the first Indo-Pakistani war. Since then, external actors have sought to mediate and resolve the conflict.

The United Nations has played a prominent role in attempting to settle the dispute. In 1948, the UN Security Council passed a resolution calling for a ceasefire and a plebiscite to determine the future of Kashmir. However, due to differing interpretations of the resolution and subsequent geopolitical dynamics, the plebiscite has never been held.

Over the years, various countries and organizations have offered their assistance as mediators. The United States, the United Kingdom, and China have all made efforts to facilitate dialogue between India and Pakistan. Additionally, the Organization of Islamic Cooperation (OIC) has voiced its support for the rights of the Kashmiri people and called for a peaceful resolution.

Religious leaders have also played a role in the conflict. Both India and Pakistan have sought the support of religious communities to bolster their claims over Kashmir. This has further fueled tensions and hindered efforts towards reconciliation.

The external involvement in the Kashmir conflict has had a profound impact on the region. The disputed territory has become heavily militarized, with both India and Pakistan deploying troops along the Line of Control. This militarization has resulted in numerous military confrontations and wars, causing immense suffering for the people of Kashmir.

Efforts towards peace and reconciliation have been ongoing. Track II diplomacy, involving non-governmental organizations and individuals, has sought to facilitate dialogue and build trust between India and Pakistan. Confidence-building measures, such as cross-border trade and cultural exchanges, have also been implemented to promote peace in the region.

In conclusion, the Kashmir conflict has seen significant external involvement, with various countries, organizations, and religious leaders attempting to mediate and resolve the dispute. However, the complexity of the conflict and the deeply entrenched positions of India and Pakistan have made a lasting resolution elusive. Diplomats, mediators, and religious leaders must continue to work towards peace and reconciliation in the region, taking into account the historical context, cultural and religious differences, and economic rivalry between the two nations. Only through sustained efforts and international cooperation can a peaceful resolution to the Kashmir conflict be achieved.

Chapter 6: Military Confrontations and Wars between India and Pakistan

Indo-Pakistani wars of 1947-1948 and 1965

The Indo-Pakistani wars of 1947-1948 and 1965 are pivotal events in the history of the India-Pakistan conflict. These conflicts have shaped the relationship between the two nations and have had far-reaching consequences for the region. In this subchapter, we will delve into the causes, outcomes, and implications of these wars, addressing the diplomats, mediators, and religious leaders who play a crucial role in resolving conflicts and promoting peace.

The Indo-Pakistani war of 1947-1948 marked the first armed conflict between the newly independent nations of India and Pakistan. It was triggered by the dispute over the princely state of Jammu and Kashmir, which had a majority Muslim population but a Hindu ruler. The war resulted in the division of the state and the establishment of the Line of Control, which continues to be a contentious issue today. This conflict highlighted the border disputes and territorial conflicts that have plagued India-Pakistan relations since their inception.

The war of 1965 further intensified the enmity between India and Pakistan. It was primarily fought over the disputed region of Kashmir, but underlying cultural and religious differences also fueled the conflict. India, with its Hindu majority, and Pakistan, with its Muslim majority, found themselves in a bitter struggle for dominance. The war ended in a stalemate, but it further deepened the animosity between the two nations.

Both these wars were influenced by the historical context of the India-Pakistan conflict. The legacy of British colonialism, which partitioned the subcontinent along religious lines, played a significant role in shaping their relations. The economic rivalry and competition between India and Pakistan also contributed to the escalation of tensions.

Moreover, the nuclear arms race between the two nations added a dangerous dimension to the conflict. The possession of nuclear weapons by both India and Pakistan has increased the stakes and made the resolution of disputes even more critical.

International interventions and mediation have played a crucial role in attempting to resolve the India-Pakistan conflict. The United Nations and other countries have made numerous efforts to facilitate peace talks and negotiations between the two nations. The impact of these interventions and the role they can play in achieving lasting peace will be explored in this subchapter.

Lastly, we will examine the impact of the India-Pakistan conflict on the Kashmir region. The ongoing dispute over Kashmir has resulted in decades of violence and instability, causing immense suffering for the people living in the region. Understanding the consequences of this conflict is essential for developing effective strategies for peace and reconciliation.

In conclusion, the Indo-Pakistani wars of 1947-1948 and 1965 have had a profound impact on the India-Pakistan conflict. The historical, cultural, religious, and economic factors fueling the enmity between the two nations will be explored, along with the role of international interventions, the nuclear arms race, and the impact on the Kashmir region. A comprehensive understanding of these conflicts is crucial for diplomats, mediators, and religious leaders to contribute to efforts towards peace and reconciliation between India and Pakistan.

The Bangladesh Liberation War and its impact on India-Pakistan relations

The Bangladesh Liberation War of 1971 was a pivotal event in the history of the India-Pakistan conflict, with profound implications for the region and its key stakeholders. This subchapter explores the historical context, territorial conflicts, cultural differences, and the role of British colonialism in shaping India-Pakistan relations. It also delves into the economic rivalry, nuclear arms race, international interventions, and the impact of the conflict on the Kashmir region. Finally, it highlights the military confrontations, as well as the efforts towards peace and reconciliation between India and Pakistan.

The Bangladesh Liberation War emerged from the deep-rooted political and cultural differences between East and West Pakistan. The East Pakistani population, feeling marginalized and oppressed, demanded autonomy and eventually independence. India, witnessing the plight of their Bengali-speaking brethren, provided assistance to the liberation movement, leading to a full-scale armed conflict between India and Pakistan.

The war had a profound impact on India-Pakistan relations. It further exacerbated the enmity between the two nations, as Pakistan perceived India's intervention as an act of aggression. The conflict also strained the already fragile trust between India and Pakistan, leading to a breakdown in diplomatic relations.

The Bangladesh Liberation War also highlighted the territorial disputes that have plagued India-Pakistan relations for decades. The conflict centered around East Pakistan's secession, resulting in the formation of Bangladesh. This territorial division only deepened the rift between the two nations.

Cultural and religious differences played a significant role in fueling the enmity between India and Pakistan during this period. The predominantly Muslim West Pakistan's discriminatory policies against the Bengali-speaking East Pakistani population further exacerbated the tensions and led to a sense of alienation.

British colonialism also played a crucial role in shaping India-Pakistan relations. The partition of British India in 1947, along religious lines, created the foundation for the conflict. The hastily drawn borders and the subsequent mass migration of Hindus and Muslims resulted in communal violence and deep-seated animosity.

The economic rivalry and competition between India and Pakistan added another layer of complexity to the conflict. Both nations sought to establish economic dominance and secure vital resources, leading to trade disputes and economic sanctions.

Furthermore, the nuclear arms race between India and Pakistan escalated tensions and raised the stakes of the conflict. The acquisition of nuclear weapons by both nations introduced a new dimension of fear and instability to their already strained relations.

International interventions and mediation attempts have been crucial in mitigating the conflict between India and Pakistan. The United Nations, along with various mediators, has played a significant role in facilitating dialogues and promoting peace initiatives between the two nations.

The India-Pakistan conflict has had a profound impact on the Kashmir region. The disputed territory has been a major flashpoint, with both nations engaging in military confrontations and wars over its control. The conflict has resulted in the loss of countless lives and created a humanitarian crisis in the region.

Despite the adversarial history, efforts towards peace and reconciliation between India and Pakistan have been ongoing. Diplomatic dialogues, confidence-building measures, and peace initiatives have been undertaken to resolve the conflict and usher in stability to the region.

In conclusion, the Bangladesh Liberation War had a lasting impact on India-Pakistan relations. The conflict highlighted the historical context, territorial disputes, cultural differences, and the role of British colonialism in shaping the enmity between the two nations. The economic rivalry, nuclear arms race, international interventions, and the conflict's impact on the

Kashmir region further complicated the relationship. However, efforts towards peace and reconciliation continue to offer hope for a more stable and harmonious future between India and Pakistan.

Kargil conflict and its aftermath

Title: Kargil Conflict and its Aftermath: A Turning Point in India-Pakistan Relations

The Kargil conflict, which took place between May and July 1999, marked a significant turning point in the history of the India-Pakistan conflict. This subchapter explores the causes, consequences, and the subsequent aftermath of the conflict, shedding light on its impact on various aspects of the region and its people. Addressing an audience of diplomats, mediators, and religious leaders, it aims to provide a comprehensive understanding of the conflict's implications for peace and reconciliation efforts between India and Pakistan.

The Kargil conflict emerged against the backdrop of long-standing border disputes and territorial conflicts between the two nations. It was fueled by cultural and religious differences, which intensified the enmity between India and Pakistan. Moreover, the role of British colonialism in shaping India-Pakistan relations cannot be overlooked, as it sowed the seeds of mistrust and rivalry that continue to resonate to this day.

Perhaps the most alarming aspect of the Kargil conflict was the nuclear arms race between India and Pakistan. The presence of nuclear weapons on both sides heightened tensions and raised concerns globally. International interventions and mediation played a crucial role in diffusing the situation, highlighting the need for multilateral efforts to prevent further escalation.

One of the most impacted regions in the aftermath of the Kargil conflict was Kashmir. The conflict exacerbated the already volatile situation in the region, resulting in significant loss of life and displacement. Understanding the impact on the Kashmiri people is paramount, as their aspirations for peace and stability often bear the brunt of India-Pakistan hostilities.

The conflict also led to a reevaluation of military confrontations and wars between India and Pakistan. Efforts towards peace and reconciliation gained momentum, as both nations recognized the futility of continued hostility. The Kargil conflict served as a catalyst for renewed diplomatic engagement, urging leaders to explore avenues for peaceful resolutions.

In conclusion, the Kargil conflict served as a wake-up call for both India and Pakistan, forcing them to reassess their approach to the long-standing enmity. The fallout from this conflict highlights the need for sustained efforts towards peace and reconciliation, especially in the context of the Kashmir region. Diplomats, mediators, and religious leaders must recognize the significance of the Kargil conflict in shaping the India-Pakistan conflict and work towards fostering understanding and dialogue between the two nations. Only through collective efforts can we hope to build a future of peace and stability in the region.

Chapter 7: Efforts towards Peace and Reconciliation between India and Pakistan

Track II diplomacy and people-to-people initiatives

Track II diplomacy and people-to-people initiatives have emerged as crucial tools in promoting peace and reconciliation between India and Pakistan. In this subchapter, we explore the significance and impact of these initiatives in the context of the long-standing conflict between the two nations.

Track II diplomacy, also known as informal diplomacy, involves non-governmental actors such as retired diplomats, academics, and experts engaging in dialogue and negotiations to address the underlying issues of the conflict. This form of diplomacy complements official government channels, providing a platform for open and frank discussions that may not be possible in formal settings. By fostering trust, understanding, and empathy, Track II diplomacy creates an environment conducive to resolving complex disputes.

People-to-people initiatives, on the other hand, focus on bridging the gap between the citizens of India and Pakistan. These initiatives aim to promote cultural exchange, build relationships, and promote mutual understanding among the people of both countries. Such initiatives include cultural exchanges, student exchange programs, and sports events, which help to humanize the "other" and break down stereotypes and prejudices.

In the context of the India-Pakistan conflict, Track II diplomacy and people-to-people initiatives have played a significant role in fostering dialogue and creating an atmosphere of trust. These initiatives allow for the exploration of shared historical and cultural narratives, highlighting commonalities and dispelling misconceptions. By engaging in constructive discussions, participants can identify areas of mutual interest, such as economic cooperation, trade, and joint ventures.

Furthermore, Track II diplomacy and people-to-people initiatives have the potential to address the deep-rooted issues that fuel the enmity between India and Pakistan. By acknowledging and addressing cultural and religious differences, these initiatives can promote tolerance, empathy, and respect for diversity. This, in turn, can help to mitigate the deep-seated mistrust and animosity that has plagued the relationship between the two nations.

While Track II diplomacy and people-to-people initiatives cannot replace official government negotiations, they provide a valuable supplementary approach to conflict resolution. By involving a broader range of stakeholders, including diplomats, mediators, and religious leaders, these initiatives can help create a more inclusive and holistic approach to peacebuilding.

In conclusion, Track II diplomacy and people-to-people initiatives hold immense potential in fostering peace and reconciliation between India and Pakistan. By addressing the historical, cultural, and economic dimensions of the conflict, these initiatives contribute to building trust, understanding, and empathy. As diplomats, mediators, and religious leaders, it is crucial to support and promote these initiatives to pave the way for a more peaceful and cooperative future between these two fighting brothers.

Bilateral talks and peace agreements

Bilateral talks and peace agreements have played a crucial role in the India-Pakistan conflict, as they have provided a platform for both countries to engage in dialogue and find peaceful solutions to their disputes. In this subchapter, we will explore the importance of these talks and the impact they have had on the long-standing conflict.

Throughout history, India and Pakistan have engaged in numerous bilateral talks and peace agreements in an attempt to resolve their differences and establish lasting peace. These discussions have been facilitated by diplomats, mediators, and religious leaders who understand the intricacies of the conflict and are committed to finding common ground.

One of the key elements that these talks have addressed is the historical context of the India-Pakistan conflict. By delving into the roots of the enmity between the two nations, diplomats and mediators aim to understand the deep-seated grievances and address them in a constructive manner.

Border disputes and territorial conflicts have been at the core of the India-Pakistan conflict. Bilateral talks have provided a platform to discuss these issues and negotiate mutually acceptable resolutions. By focusing on these disputes, diplomats and mediators have been able to foster an environment of understanding and compromise.

Cultural and religious differences have also fueled the enmity between India and Pakistan. Through bilateral talks, religious leaders have played a crucial role in bridging these gaps and promoting tolerance and understanding between the two nations.

The role of British colonialism in shaping India-Pakistan relations cannot be ignored. Bilateral talks have examined the historical legacy of colonialism and its impact on the current conflict. By understanding this context, diplomats and mediators have been able to navigate the complex dynamics between the two nations.

Economic rivalry and competition have also played a significant role in the India-Pakistan conflict. Bilateral talks have focused on finding ways to promote economic cooperation and reduce tensions. By exploring avenues for collaboration, diplomats and mediators have sought to shift the focus from rivalry to mutual benefit.

The nuclear arms race between India and Pakistan has added another layer of complexity to the conflict. Bilateral talks have aimed to address the concerns and fears associated with nuclear weapons and work towards disarmament and non-proliferation.

International interventions and mediation have played a crucial role in facilitating bilateral talks and peace agreements. By bringing in neutral parties, diplomats and mediators have been able to provide an unbiased perspective and guide the discussions towards productive outcomes.

The impact of the India-Pakistan conflict on the Kashmir region cannot be overstated. Bilateral talks have focused on finding a peaceful and equitable resolution to the Kashmir dispute, taking into account the aspirations and rights of the people of the region.

Despite the military confrontations and wars that have plagued India and Pakistan, there have been consistent efforts towards peace and reconciliation. Bilateral talks have provided a platform for these efforts and have resulted in significant breakthroughs, such as the Shimla Agreement and the Lahore Declaration.

In conclusion, bilateral talks and peace agreements have played a crucial role in the India-Pakistan conflict. They have provided a platform for dialogue, understanding, and compromise, and have laid the foundation for a peaceful resolution to the long-standing enmity between the two nations. Through the efforts of diplomats, mediators, and religious leaders, there is hope for a future of peace and cooperation between India and Pakistan.

Challenges and prospects for lasting peace between India and Pakistan

Introduction:

The subchapter titled "Challenges and Prospects for Lasting Peace between India and Pakistan" explores the complex and tumultuous history of the India-Pakistan conflict. Addressed to diplomats, mediators, and religious leaders, this content aims to shed light on the various factors that have hindered peaceful relations between the two nations while also highlighting the potential prospects for a lasting resolution.

Historical Context:

To understand the challenges faced by India and Pakistan, it is crucial to delve into their historical context. The enmity between these "Fighting Brothers" has deep roots, stemming from the partition of British India in 1947. The subcontinent's borders and territorial disputes have been a constant source of contention, leading to numerous military confrontations and wars.

Cultural and Religious Differences:

The cultural and religious differences between India and Pakistan have further fueled the enmity. The subchapter explores how these differences have been manipulated by various political and religious factions to maintain hostility and prevent reconciliation.

Role of British Colonialism:

British colonialism played a pivotal role in shaping India-Pakistan relations. The content examines how the British divide-and-rule policy sowed the seeds of mistrust and animosity, leaving a lasting impact on the two nations' relationship.

Economic Rivalry and Competition:

The subchapter discusses the economic rivalry and competition between India and Pakistan, which has often overshadowed any attempts at peaceful coexistence. The quest for resources, trade dominance, and regional influence has perpetuated the conflict.

Nuclear Arms Race:

The content highlights the dangerous nuclear arms race between India and Pakistan, which poses a grave threat not only to the two nations but also to regional and global security. The subchapter emphasizes the urgent need for disarmament negotiations and confidence-building measures.

Role of International Interventions and Mediation:

Efforts by the international community to mediate and resolve the India-Pakistan conflict are explored in this section. The subchapter discusses the successes and failures of various diplomatic initiatives and emphasizes the importance of sustained international engagement.

Impact on the Kashmir Region:

The India-Pakistan conflict has had a profound impact on the disputed region of Kashmir. This section examines the long-standing issue of Kashmir, its implications on regional stability, and the need for a comprehensive resolution that respects the aspirations of its people.

Efforts Towards Peace and Reconciliation:

Despite the challenges, the subchapter concludes on a hopeful note, highlighting the various efforts made towards peace and reconciliation between India and Pakistan. It explores the potential prospects for lasting peace and emphasizes the role of diplomacy, dialogue, and mutual understanding in achieving this goal.

Conclusion:

In conclusion, this subchapter provides a comprehensive analysis of the challenges and prospects for lasting peace between India and Pakistan. It aims to equip diplomats, mediators, and religious leaders with a deeper understanding of the complexities surrounding the conflict, while also inspiring them to actively contribute to the pursuit of peace and reconciliation between these two nations.

Conclusion: The Future of India-Pakistan Relations and the Role of Diplomats, Mediators, and Religious Leaders.

Conclusion: The Future of India-Pakistan Relations and the Role of Diplomats, Mediators, and Religious Leaders

The history of the India-Pakistan conflict has been marred by deep-rooted enmity, border disputes, and religious and cultural differences. It is a complex and multifaceted issue that requires the attention and efforts of various stakeholders, including diplomats, mediators, and religious leaders. As we conclude our exploration of the conflict in "Brothers at War: A History of the India-Pakistan Conflict," it is crucial to reflect on the future of India-Pakistan relations and the potential roles these key individuals can play in fostering peace and reconciliation.

Diplomats have a significant responsibility in facilitating dialogue and negotiations between India and Pakistan. They possess the diplomatic skills and expertise necessary to bridge the divide and find common ground. By encouraging open and honest communication, diplomats can work towards resolving border disputes and territorial conflicts. Additionally, they can play a vital role in addressing the economic rivalry and competition between the two nations, by promoting trade and cooperation that benefits both sides.

Mediators, on the other hand, can bring impartiality and neutrality to the table. They can act as facilitators, guiding the dialogue between India and Pakistan towards peaceful resolutions. Their expertise in conflict resolution and mediation techniques can help both nations overcome their differences and build a foundation for long-term peace.

Religious leaders also have a crucial role to play in the India-Pakistan conflict. Given that much of the enmity is fueled by cultural and religious differences, religious leaders can promote tolerance, understanding, and respect among their followers. By emphasizing the shared values and principles of their respective religions, they can help break down barriers and foster a sense of unity and coexistence.

International interventions and mediation efforts have had both positive and negative impacts on the India-Pakistan conflict. While external involvement can provide much-needed support and resources, it is imperative that such interventions are carried out with sensitivity and respect for the sovereignty of both nations. Effective international mediation should focus on creating an environment conducive to dialogue and negotiation, rather than imposing solutions from external sources.

The impact of the India-Pakistan conflict on the Kashmir region cannot be understated. It has resulted in prolonged violence and instability, with significant humanitarian consequences. Efforts towards peace and reconciliation must prioritize the well-being and aspirations of the people of Kashmir. The involvement of diplomats, mediators, and religious leaders can contribute to creating a more inclusive and sustainable peace process that takes into account the aspirations and grievances of all stakeholders.

In conclusion, the future of India-Pakistan relations rests on the shoulders of diplomats, mediators, and religious leaders. Their collective efforts can help overcome historical animosities, resolve territorial disputes, bridge cultural and religious differences, and promote economic cooperation. By working together, these key individuals can pave the way for a peaceful and prosperous future for both nations and the Kashmir region. It is a challenging task, but one that holds immense potential for positive change.

SPECIAL CHAPTER: The Nuclear Capabilities of India and Pakistan

The nuclear capabilities of India

India has a diverse and evolving nuclear program that has been shaped by both its strategic considerations and its aspirations as a major power. Here's a brief overview as of my last training cut-off in January 2022:

1. **Historical Context**: India's nuclear program began in the late 1940s. While initially focused on peaceful uses of nuclear energy, by the 1960s, India began to explore the possibility of a weapons program. The 1974 "Smiling Buddha" test marked India's first nuclear detonation, which New Delhi called a "peaceful nuclear explosion."

2. **Weapons Arsenal**: By 2022, India is believed to possess around 150 to 160 nuclear warheads. India has a policy of "credible minimum deterrence," which means it maintains a nuclear arsenal sufficient to deter adversaries but doesn't seek parity with nuclear superpowers.

3. **Doctrine and No First Use (NFU) Policy**: India follows a No First Use policy, meaning it has pledged not to use nuclear weapons unless first attacked by an adversary using nuclear weapons. However, discussions periodically arise within the strategic community about the viability and credibility of the NFU policy in the changing geopolitical environment.

4. **Delivery Systems**: India has a triad of delivery systems – land-based ballistic missiles, aircraft, and sea-based assets. Notable among them are:
   - **Land**: Agni series of missiles, with the Agni-V having a range that can cover most of Asia and parts of Europe and Africa.
   - **Air**: Aircraft like the Mirage 2000 and Sukhoi Su-30MKI can be equipped with nuclear bombs.
   - **Sea**: The INS Arihant, India's first indigenous nuclear-powered submarine, became operational, marking the beginning of India's sea-based deterrent.
5. **Civilian Nuclear Program**: India is also keen on expanding its civilian nuclear energy program. After the 2008 India-U.S. civil nuclear agreement, India gained access to international nuclear markets for civilian purposes while retaining its military nuclear program.
6. **International Stance**: India is not a signatory to the Nuclear Non-Proliferation Treaty (NPT) but asserts its commitment to global nuclear disarmament. The country has a strong track record of non-proliferation. India is keen to join export control regimes like the Nuclear Suppliers Group (NSG), but its non-NPT status has been a sticking point.
7. **Regional Dynamics**: India's nuclear strategy is heavily influenced by its regional dynamics, especially its relationships with Pakistan and China. Both these nations possess nuclear weapons, leading to a complex

strategic environment in South Asia and the broader Asian region.

8. **Safety and Security**: India has invested significantly in the safety and security of its nuclear arsenal, infrastructure, and facilities. The country has strict controls and protocols to prevent any unauthorized use or accidental detonations.

In summary, India's nuclear capabilities are influenced by a combination of regional strategic concerns, global ambitions, and a commitment to maintaining a credible deterrent. The nation continues to evolve its capabilities in line with its perceived threats and global standing. However, like all nuclear-armed nations, India faces the challenge of ensuring that its nuclear arsenal remains a tool of deterrence and not actual conflict.

The nuclear capabilities of Pakistan

Pakistan is a significant nuclear player in South Asia, and its nuclear program has been a key aspect of its defense and strategic posture, particularly concerning its eastern neighbor, India. Here's a brief overview of Pakistan's nuclear capabilities as of January 2022:

1. **Historical Development**: Pakistan began its pursuit of nuclear technology in the 1970s, driven by concerns over India's nuclear program and the perceived need to counterbalance it. In response to India's 1974 nuclear test (often referred to as the "Smiling Buddha"), Pakistan accelerated its efforts. The country conducted

its first nuclear tests in 1998, just weeks after India's second series of nuclear tests.

2. **Weapons Arsenal**: As of 2022, it's estimated that Pakistan possesses around 165 to 175 nuclear warheads. There has been a consistent effort to modernize and expand its arsenal, which is slightly larger than India's, according to various estimates.

3. **Doctrine**: Unlike India, Pakistan has not publicly adopted a "No First Use" policy. Its strategic posture is centered around deterring India, and because of the conventional military imbalance with India, Pakistan has hinted at a willingness to use nuclear weapons first if it believes that a conventional conflict might threaten the state's integrity.

4. **Delivery Systems**:
    - **Land**: Pakistan's ballistic missiles, like the Shaheen and Ghauri series, are notable components of its delivery mechanism.
    - **Air**: The Pakistan Air Force's aircraft, like the F-16, can be equipped to deliver nuclear weapons.
    - **Sea**: Pakistan has been working on a sea-based leg of its nuclear triad, with developments like the Babur-3 submarine-launched cruise missile, signaling its nascent sea-based deterrence capability.

5. **Civilian Nuclear Program**: While Pakistan's civilian nuclear program isn't as advanced as some other countries', it does operate nuclear power plants with China's assistance. This collaboration has been a

significant factor in the growth of Pakistan's civilian nuclear energy infrastructure.

6. **International Relations**: Pakistan, like India, is not a signatory to the Nuclear Non-Proliferation Treaty (NPT). However, it seeks to join the Nuclear Suppliers Group (NSG), like India, but faces challenges due to its non-NPT status and past proliferation issues, particularly the A.Q. Khan network scandal.

7. **Safety and Security**: Pakistan's control over its nuclear arsenal and the safety of its facilities are crucial concerns, especially given the country's internal security challenges. Pakistan has, however, made significant efforts to ensure the security of its nuclear assets, creating a robust command and control system under the National Command Authority.

8. **Regional Dynamics**: The interplay between Pakistan and India, both nuclear-armed neighbors with historical tensions, creates a unique and complex regional nuclear dynamic. The presence of militant groups in the region, along with unresolved territorial disputes like Kashmir, adds layers of complexity.

In summary, Pakistan's nuclear capabilities are shaped by its strategic environment, especially its relationship with India. It has developed a diverse range of delivery systems and an expanding arsenal, which is seen by many as an effort to maintain a credible deterrent against perceived threats. As with all nuclear-armed states, ensuring that nuclear weapons remain tools of deterrence and not actual use is a paramount challenge.

Comparison between the nuclear capabilities of India and Pakistan

India and Pakistan are neighboring countries with a history of conflicts and tensions, and both are nuclear-armed states. Their respective nuclear programs and strategies have been shaped by regional dynamics, especially their bilateral relationship. Here's a comparative overview of the nuclear capabilities of India and Pakistan as of 2022:

1. **Historical Development**:
    - **India**: Started its nuclear program in the late 1940s, initially for peaceful purposes. Conducted its first nuclear test in 1974, named "Smiling Buddha."
    - **Pakistan**: Began its nuclear efforts in the 1970s, significantly driven by India's 1974 test. Conducted its own nuclear tests in 1998, soon after India's second set of tests.

2. **Weapons Arsenal**:
    - **India**: Estimated to possess around 150 to 160 nuclear warheads.
    - **Pakistan**: Estimated to have slightly more, around 165 to 175 nuclear warheads.

3. **Doctrine**:
    - **India**: Adopts a "No First Use" (NFU) policy, meaning it pledges not to use nuclear weapons unless first attacked with them.
    - **Pakistan**: Has not adopted a public NFU policy and has a posture that leans more

toward early use in a conflict, especially given its conventional military disparity with India.

4. **Delivery Systems**:
   - **India**: Possesses a nuclear triad, which includes land-based missiles (like the Agni series), aircraft (such as the Mirage 2000 and Sukhoi Su-30MKI), and sea-based assets (like the INS Arihant submarine).
   - **Pakistan**: Has land-based missiles (like the Shaheen and Ghauri series) and aircraft (like the F-16). It's also developing sea-based capabilities with missiles like the Babur-3.

5. **Civilian Nuclear Program**:
   - **India**: Has an advanced civilian program, bolstered by the 2008 India-U.S. civil nuclear deal that allowed access to international nuclear markets.
   - **Pakistan**: Operates nuclear power plants mainly with China's assistance and seeks to expand its civilian nuclear infrastructure.

6. **International Relations**:
   - **India**: Not a signatory to the Nuclear Non-Proliferation Treaty (NPT) but seeks to join the Nuclear Suppliers Group (NSG) and has a strong non-proliferation record.
   - **Pakistan**: Also not an NPT signatory and aims to join the NSG. However, its bid is complicated by past proliferation concerns, especially linked to the A.Q. Khan network.

7. **Safety and Security**:
    ◦ **India**: Has invested heavily in the safety and security of its nuclear arsenal and infrastructure.
    ◦ **Pakistan**: Given internal security challenges, there are concerns about the safety of its nuclear assets. However, Pakistan has established a robust command and control system under its National Command Authority to secure its arsenal.

8. **Regional Dynamics**:
    ◦ Both countries have a complex nuclear relationship, with the Kashmir dispute being a primary point of contention. The presence of nuclear weapons on both sides has introduced a new dimension to their strategic calculations, with some arguing that it has introduced a form of stability, while others believe it has made the region more volatile.

In summary, while both India and Pakistan possess significant nuclear capabilities, their doctrines, delivery systems, and international engagements differ based on their strategic priorities and perceptions. The nuclear backdrop in South Asia is a critical component of global nuclear politics and remains a focal point for concerns around nuclear escalation and diplomacy.

9 798822 368224 0